Face Before Against

Isabelle Garron

Face Before Against

ISBN: 978-1-933959-04-7

COVER ART
"Tender Star" by Carrie Moyer

DESIGN
HvA Design, New York

Litmus Press is the publishing program of Ether Sea Projects, Inc., a 501 (c) (3)
nonprofit literature and arts organization dedicated to supporting innovative, cross-
genre writing with an emphasis on poetry and international works in translation.

Face Before Against is made possible by public funds from the New York State Council
on the Arts, a state agency. Litmus Press is also supported by grants from the
Council of Literary Magazines and Presses and individual donors. All contributions
are tax-deductible to the extent allowed by law.

State of the Arts

NYSCA

Litmus Press
PO Box 25526
Brooklyn, NY 11202-5526
www.litmuspress.org

Face Before Against is distributed by
Small Press Distribution
1341 Seventh Street
Berkeley, CA 94710
www.spdbooks.org

TABLE OF CONTENTS

Drawn back forcibly to my estate.

Danielle COLLOBERT

overseas

under an X
yesterday's eye
of the needle
impact of seven
wars and according to
the number

overseas

masks   sutures
bends. to the eye
suddenly naked

the rupture
in portrait

slope where
yours of April
was made

sign of more
than mourning

Day of your armor
on the table

night fell
before that attack

The mouth
snatches

the truth out
of our hands.

your name
in the latium.

In the square
a tuft of grass

refuge between
two cobblestones.

a dealer
paces the quay

a boy
looks for a boy

a man
has already given

another comes who
doesn't move you.

Scene
far

high
sets

anima
even

tack
around

your green look
like his
   miscast
coming from the corridor.

Seen

. on the strewn hay
of the serfs'
pantheon

– and the murky water
inside a glass
in the kitchen sun.

Voice

strangled
– avocado pit
soon ripe –

sprouted growth
. housed
in the bone structure.

View   adjoined

four   matches
. a sure gesture
– neat a lone –
fell into place in an emptiness

. and the plenary attendance
– until disturbance is reached –

Voice   stinging / so

. voice squirting
like fruit
between the fingers

. today
impaled

voice   and law / also

. who marry
– ordinarily with
the fires extinguished –

the heat
and the growth

Voice   noxious / rushed

. one day of per
person   and less
than five   articles

– in all
and for all

voice.   wax serum
powder lance pass
/ and body tensor

          / and tension fire

        . you who stoke it
        sowing the rushes

        just as well
       . snatch my lot

(b) my lot
as well   which strikes you
in turn   some wishes
. crossed out false

– on   a dance
 card   mottled
 the other Sunday

– me   so little / lodged
 in your heels
. what a picture!

Family
lodging   basketwork
from / the country

. decidedly
I will have seen it all
in disarray

to the perse eyes
of the gypsies
– and without a shadow

and so since!
. in this common
calm / repeating

also. how the evening
the steam from soup
blurs / the night

so that. under my finger
an announcement. on
the glass / squeaks

.... in the absence of the aged
welcomed by the mother

.   the mothers

work ended
under the paradigmatic

– scents

"Push push
keep the mask"
says the voice

thinking millstones. touches.
rose-flare fevers
unique   stroke

and you
– better than a country

. you *Muscat Trellis*
: dwelling and sign
from where perhaps starts

the sensitive point
. my genuflections
that's to say

. ... for the brine
watch the time
of the first bath

rinse the basin
with a lot of water
. not to forget

the sweet almond
oil   against
. the cracks

[Closing of the site
. she stays   seated
in the steps' descent

        ] instead of climbing
        – she retakes this open
        blue   *a capella*

/ dunes
traveler
dormant   streams

      . loose   half
      – and full face   even
      . thrown / on the register

voice   vaned
– high
      . achieved
in the compressor

voice   of a thousand
and one languages
. voice   of voices

mistress
. under the lava

voices inside
– bond outside

. which / capsized
for a word
– succumbs

and you. dear
like that
to their diverse objects

call forth. insert
well / . if dropped body

there is

call out
climb as high
heave and tack
that one

by a bone
as you say with
your author's
smile

Call forth you
who   deprived of air
and of water

        has fled – reached
       . before the story

       – disguise before
       against   and soon

       / cut . clean

(Scarcely morning)
. continuous voice
– cradles from calling

. sleeps injured
– in the off-season
why the heart

released pheasants

[encampment
at your feet
supple earth.

the war. slicing
– these stories –

        these advances
        into the scenery

        . breakwater to your
        faults since / when
        a world   would be

a world
. dodecaphonic

a world
of new voices
. rushed onto the escalator

a world
. or decidedly
a dismayed crowd

. a man / woman before
who ruthlessly looks on
hears . nothing

    . of this
    slacking love

       . . . . .

there] since the following
. spinners since
the female   song

there] from the shed until
the trails hollowed out by
the marine   shepherds

there]   lashing and furled
. rasping yesterday

now / skies
and he .   becomes line

voice. contrary
to forces

. (track
of five steps)

even . attached
– documentary

     weds
     simplified

          – the night
          lasting
          the night –

voices before
canvas. together
biting face.

voice against
veil .   rings
white. and setting

voices
squared.

blue background
. before

said again
. and so my voice
– will be that   which
under a wind   floats

. against / will float

against   the no
voice of the breather
pointing the quill

the stage chewed
of the nosh

act one
(as : *enclosure*)

      the fishermen
      leaning

      in the sorrow
      of fates
      handling the bowline

scene two
(as : *bite*)

        the tanners
        equipped

        : strap under the forge
        like hoe
        in the dream

Blacksmiths' adventure.
woven suites.
fishermen of fates.

. ... ..

in this way hoe. when
the embrace. overthrow
matador.

. ... ..

Pre-Columbian angelus.

    they will re-enter
by the harbor.

     a trophy
in hand.

. ... ..

The one will be taken
           by violent
pains
           – in the sides

near to the remarkable –

He will collapse
. unruffled . tattooed

Following
from then
. will be

                    . will be faults
                    enlarged : all
                    the acres counted.

               . will be. empty
               hours : slow distillation
               of the fermenting fruits

will be
here-hers
plus one

      at the modal imprecation
      came to suspend
      . and against which

. slip against luff
. wave cut
– prediction

. an arrangement with
what disappears
– under the waves

Woven suites
American Indian chant

woven
– American Indian
. my suites

murderous
. yesterday arched
– burning Sumer

        chant   of Kubatum
        chant   of Shu Sin

        lovers.   in the marvel
        that would become   their end

One will find   their story
after some years.

Tablets. wax
 lost in paraphs
– testaments

Laws rewritten
by the squatting
executor

simplifying the opprobrium

of the same . the trace
of an inflection of bone

not in the dead

. ...

and as to the previous day
– identical –

between the steps
leading to the sepulchers

another should   make
the discovery   of matrixes

frames streaked
uterine in the clay
sliding   in the recesses.
tomorrow   hoisted facing.
and as.

and as when I
. sleep   clutched
private   .placed bodily
divided   apart
of a legible   .non-
pain

History is constructed
so.

Since it happens
today   that it   comes
all decomposed

a face
enters.

– a man
holds himself straight.

a mango
in a bowl

clear
a bit by taste

from my forgetting
– to split.

partition and. coda
that which fixed plan
– four color

verify excavation
. infiltration of waters

.. ...

one marks
        from a motif's angle
the shade of forsythias.

on a remnant of serge
        a kind of fibula
/ broken

        – finally   from where
she is   taken

unfurlage

I.

neutral to the double
face of the peak

just added   late
in life   to cliffs
the day's seven lights

and if not that
. of some other night

grasp
incomplete
. frequent

/ at a slant

Neutrality of a double
point of falling
arming the bodies

against. the
voices' quality
through the empiric

that   inspires

.   ...   ..

Even if
diceless
a single man
sleeps and sees

on the footpath
the water diviner
pauses
numb

separation   between
gods. .....
amateur order
of some exhibitions.

Suddenly
dances return
. ... ..

return twinned
to curves and their sound
. ... ..

                              its hairless   rhythm
                         and bracing vibrations

                              for two hands
                           in the sticky filets.

the left one at water's
edge   even while
advancing   drops

the measure
          of your good
and butts

    against the hull
the recalcitrant link.

We can read
likewise
in the opuscule

"moorings
 revelry of the watch
 joy of the drowned"

. ... ..

I kept some   on me
. against the wars

the love
of notes

our fingers interwoven
at the bow

on the field
of honor

. ... ..

emanating   from others
knife gestures

"entitle   understand
the prompter   the spinning wheel

avoid the broken bone
on some days the splint"

. ....

you come. from elsewhere

from behind.   to walk
on the rubble   in labor's space

to fear   before even age

an all unfurled

II.

enter in
the station
/

      "twice
       attempt
       the parallel"

descending to the port
of Genoa embarking
before the Byzantine Hymen

it was the idyll . dead

I saw from here
your Palermitani offer
I was bareheaded

I watched . just

outside in hand
a slice of watermelon
morning at the hotel

with this feeling

but you ... ..

at high tide   toward
       the north weary   you

still had
subtlized the layer
             of shade   on the bay

             except he is remarkable
             and I against   since
                          forever.   *with nothing.*

                          •

so   what proves to be
it's   following the flow
as   removing the fire

on the verge of igniting

between rock and enamel
jade and flock
azulejos and fountain

the   hands one
time anew
joined in the blues

yours
. of you

you / slight
wild ones.   close
up to detention

. you   . you   . you

you   be
the aged   two

of all
left from a body
in the mouth

while running.   aspired
/ magisterial

the ground
covered with rain

mockeries spread
. other   reds
cutanaceous

so definitely his
at depth

. to this point
he must
/

that he must
read nonetheless

. on a way
– with liaisons

. and distinguish
in the echo

charm
recitation
of leaps

cadence   poured
like wax
split wood
spelling   of some colors

step /   in a forum

As such / outside
the gynaeceum   open
text   .time
in passage

over a white
sheet   ancient
until the daughters'
betrayal   .nteenth
of the bed

defeat
to remind me
she deciphered
visible   to loss

to loss
as much to say
lost ego

. Venetian
as in Bombay
during the fast.

and lost. especially.
since the wild end
of S. *Tahla*

visible.
on the frontispiece
closed places
from pre-war

or
certain sorcery
seminars held
under personal order

of. the wife
of the. marquis

] at present   yes
drunk-yes to their head

. a yes says where   I
recognize the obscenity
of women not to have
anything but the odor
. of this avowal of women

a bouquet in the hand

yes   by mistake / here-below
a great poem

yes   a   poem
in the   blood
of some   periods

under mark of injury
. the cadaver's ruse

a yes of the offense
/ inept against
her word dead

. epigraphic
to who would implore
– nevertheless.

nevertheless   yes.
so as
not to

survive
it

.

III.

not to steal the rhythms

to see afresh
her body gift
the credits

turn
I beg you.
and that

first   in the eyes
of some people
here present

the avatar of a wind.

ballets
open wounds
. writings

. writings
at the first breath
of breaths
of the blackest
caverns

of a world, of one
fire of a myth of one
goddess.
. ... ..

. Etruscan   epiphanies
phallic world   to half
unfit   mundane
the evening   on the cobbled
paths say patrician

unique
women. unfastened.

married
off. in the abstraction.

finally   since
turning   around
you   will have read

     – you
     so much missed –

: Hapax
or see the yellows.

        – silks folded half-
        perennial half-
        dream.   the echo

aligned struggles
the august
walls   constructed

                   , the horns on death

You say indeed

it happened one day
it was noon. when
in their eyes. we
were. trivial
on the passages

to redo. the gestures
to not. understand
to speak. in the future
of the first language.

                besides
        in itself
        it's.   irremovable

(one hears that
in incessant returns
open fracture

but came after
only
to write it)

the train
the station
the pines

the creek.
the pillars.
beaten.

the chignon
knot face
. to the sea

the above-us
before the Island
green. and you

against. the fact
of stretching the
rigging

. the ropes
in the cleats.

the meteorology
of. this moment
– there / yes again

it's in reverse
that I think

a new year's
evening. to finish
all. to render

advancing
all the while on
a steel   track

: either distinctly
take hold of a beginning
celebrate the birthday
since it comes

or say   sluggishly
an excerpt from an inventory
. listing the peninsulas

"there was   a young
woman in the painting
such a vow

daughter of the old   medium
opening   the lock
of a trunk

the drawing   the reflection
in the mirror
of the spouses

all   seemed
even her breast
in the palm
of the painting

lit   and carrying
up   to the   face
the smile   effaced
to exult   Italian

all her breast
I say to you
and this fold here
of the fabric

twisted at the place
at the point of order
in the crucial
transparency

: such   scattering
the gift of the faun

. passed / . smitten

the topaz reef
of his well-being"

for the threading
finally. you will watch
. in second degree

the shimmering
of parts
from the stage
marked by the
dark withdrawal of a
body of your
fatigue on the
green covering   of
the sister   her
late

One must / nevertheless
– turn again
. build

– built in doubt
. before the masks
– imported

the cold under the heights

Ample solution
provisional
. and numbered

on the bedspread
. on the state of
impostures

. and this look   that contains   the other

birthday scene

who knows
who.   saw the
augur basin
smelling strongly
of fish eggs

in the flesh
orbs and walls
nidify   larvae
and dig

mold lifting
from the seasons
to her face

(slowly)   .a prehistory

With this rite

from before   the flint
scrapings. some bones   dried
around the hearth

some men

armed. back against
the wall   some writings
facing   the feminine bestiary

the genitals painted

Yesterday otherwise
facing. tabernacles
at the heart of processions

accented under the chanting.
votive.   from your mouth

– sublimity – and your hip
in mine   incarnated

.. ...

yesterday   their rumps' extravagance
on the jar necks   molded
shop woman   lascivious

abused

. ...

yesterday   in a story
a man filmed
late in the century

hallucinated

. ...

there,   at the edges
of a well near the surface
at the doors. inscribed with the place

– charred

against our Punic memories

in ink by torches

I saw.   so well.

the ocher of a horse

a ceremonial comb

. rupture connate
convex lineature

. rain and deciphering
opercula.

traces. foundations

fragments of. the written
. late palimpsest
– or a fire.   on the Aventin

Lightning on. the spouse's
waist.   she
embraces the lover

. who refuses her

Villa Giulia
Villa Borghese
Villa Adriana

Villa Cesarina
Giuletta Massina

mà   nonna ! nonna !

nonnétta
nonnétto

nonnìna
nonnìno
nònno

nonnùlla

A charm passed.

on the thread passed.
and you. Agatha.
were she.

you rejoice
in a skirt.

agatha.
on the way

agatha.
in the church

a. on a bench
near some offerings

a. breathing
with three sprigs
the lavender

a. and the famous
death. of her
favorite of the dead

initial
and old
. Indian woman

marvelous
unexpected
. so petite

agatha.
when it's sultry

a. in time
of rain.

and Notre Dame
bordered with.
Japanese cherry trees

agatha.
on Mayan ground

(show a.
picking up a
shell of a black
flower. not far
from the avenida.

    – ... the rest and end
    of Pedralbes –

    be it a. the eyes
    closed   before
    a Christ on the cross)

agatha
imagine
Isadora

Duncan

who. with Irish
origins
who. died

in Nice

the scarf
in the wheel

. Marina's body
at the end

the dance.
agatha.

sheltered
by the legs.

all the limbs
firm.

think
    of your sisters
of the bas-reliefs.

In fact it's the thunder
agatha. it's the accident.
always. what slides.

It's a passageway over   the Eden
an espresso in   Brooklyn
a dash of milk at   Pyramides stop

January.   train tracks
under some snow.   a home
less stare   at those
who pass by   the foot of the stairs

February. at the museum
ashamed facing a totem   wood language
stolen   for those who dead   will
remain far   from profanations

. from terrible profanations

crowd. on the main boulevard
you're dressed   in the grey coat
that seems both expensive   and   very poor
riches and rags
at the same time as

                    the March downpours

End of the storm   finally.

"forget the order of the letters"

take up the scene again
– said as an aside –
of the birthday

the candles
the cake
the screen

the white atmosphere
– hospit / able

scent similar
to. medicine bottles

in a blank posed   . facing the title
. the force of a woman

who with her voice   pretends   crippled
climbs   a notch   and melting
– at each gyration   of the record player

. as her shape gradually dissolves
she becomes beauty   that sells itself
– underexposed   in the installation

. Olympia's daughter

In the performance black-out
. Olympia's daughter

the fake orchid
in your hair
is not least likeness

– and your cat.

and along the slipper
with a Phoenician look
.child .child .child

. Olympia's progeny

you will see. turning
Melanesian. this belated
gesture   of a fool

The permanent
so it's said

– in the black-out
performance

– as he advances
coming back from your bed

– fife player in clogs
sent outside the frame.

a bunch of iris
a hat   in his hand

off-screen
he smokes   sitting
without getting out of character.

pensive to your shape
before the mistake
in itself   *the lovers'*
sarcophagus

on the day   never
ending   of your age

that it exudes
traverses
and memorizes

it slips out   how he's clever

you. touched
in the yellows

at the crossing
of a bridge and a plateau

          he. bruskly
          livid
          . looks like someone

     .. ...

          like this man who goes around
          without i.d.
          – from the beginning

          / at screenplay's end

note:

to delimit his subject
. according to the images
– in the deep   first

"we'll cut out distraction
and keep the disquiet"

and in the margin:

"take care of the make-up"
love is. important
despite the incidents

he will wear sandals
. she. barefoot
– will be sleeping already

Behind the hangings
the prompter will signal

– in echoing suites

the chronic call
of the false. flower deliverer

.. ...

the moment after
a beau will bring

on stage. a bride

plastic   posed
between the roses

. ... ..

Such eruption indisposes
the parties involved
facing those watching them

. but time
reverses anew

the snarl of a   wildcat

. a note   falls at the lady's feet

Sequence *spoken*
of an *actual* word
interrupted in the footage

. in pencil   an author
– anonymous   has written
these words.   under the text

:
Lucretia can't arise
with such impunity
against Judith
. "

fire not

French, color ('63). drama. / US, black & white ('62). Biography, / Brit., color ('48). Musical drama, / Franco-belgian-german, color ('90) dramatic comedy, / Brit., color ('84). Science fiction / US color (92). Dramatic comedy, / ('78 – 197 min). War drama, /Brit., color ('99 – 110 min). / Dramatic comedy,/ US color ('86 – 120 min) Crime thriller, / Italian, color. (95 min) Psychological drama, / Chinese, color ('01 – 98 min). Dramatic comedy, / French, color ('00 – 120 min). Dramatic comedy, / Danish, color ('98 – 106 min). Dramatic Comedy / US, color ('98 – 95 min) Dramatic comedy. / French, color ('62 – 27 min). Science Fiction/ US, color ('83 – 138 min.) Psychological drama, / French, black and white, color ('55 – 31 min.) Documentary / French, color ('98 – 95 min.) Erotic

drama. / French, black & white ('59 – 82 min.) Horror,

. on the ticket it's   marked
 doors close
– right at curtain   time

. bitter night   in the black
– reversed   or the whiteness
of your oval / sliced

a blind
– fine. where your
fingers pass. fine

. through the slats
– warped   giving
also on.   the garden

a milky cloud
in my tea
– thanks. in a plain voice

thanks.   in time
with the watering system
. to the one. before the one

a blind   (*pause to read*)
. as a passage

. slot to capture
written. retained

– shaft.   her
heading deleted

debated. even
demented

– measured to the depths

here and here
– and here too
. sonorous

measured to the depths

– for a few years
facing the lighthouse
time then against

from where   lengths of the bay

rounds without hour
    black under each eye
life forms
     on tree trunks
in the molting

cry of a body
familiar then ... .
unrecognizable

now. even here
feet in the clay

– lying face down
among tools

some combatants
last
        – between
our slow orders

that's to say / how
. warriors   kings
      demeaned men
you won me over
      . how I ignored it

      how one day   of one month
I could have died in Dubrovnik
      . by the force of your fist
      without believing in fate / no

. in the iron age
use of the bow

sheep shin-bone
pulled out during ploughing

curving at the neck

hand-wrought pieces
seasons of floods
. in canine position

promises of union
facing the loggias

still lives
for a novel   of another
that one fixes

at the end   of the deserts

aisle seat
. barely turned   back
to the earth   pillars

to the cinders   of a kingdom

– once the gods are sold
 it's useless   to train
 the cocks

. for money
– just for food
 to finish

. false / on the   metro
ticket (*infused white*) it's written
where I come from

and not you
since   it's clearly
this rare   ultramarine blue
that   reaches me

. even before
– all oceans

Literacy
of water

silica
soda
. alumina
of lime

. sulfur
or the azure

fire / substance
that one grinds

. depths
bends
– outer reach
of your arm

ethylic
passes

Fire not
. now

. yesterday outside
in fragments
– with missing
edges

– in this sense
that led
solidly
to set

struck then pitched
in a precise spot
. as a sign of winter's
places – desolate

often . who hostile
. who   inhabited. who
disturbed to
astonish

Fire not
. now

pronounced
– already back turned
. said before it

in a manner
insisting with those
words : female
circle   and them ....

– them : *so fine*
that I'd not

them so fine
that I'd not.

forgotten their mouth
. the fall   of their hands
– the echo of. cohorts

the adorable house

so fine
. intimacy of legs
the look   of someone
– one liked them as
if facing

so fine
that smiling
lays the shock
– a little closer
to the flexing

so fine that they
. woman's voice : the eyes,
– voix de femme : the erotic
. metaphor   times two

and at the border
– even those
  that are   and become

                  . varied / premature
                  – unthinkable yesterday
                  this evening   stretched

                  our slow orders

Retake
(/) let's go

. risk
a stroke

– in a smoky joint

retake
. yes

slowly
. very

– felted everywhere

.

Depths (1966-1980)
Depths III . Dusseldorf. 1969

depths. flames
– felt all over

flames. semen
– lead all over

depths. copper
plate   base
to fracture

. craft   wax
& slip knot
over an umber fleck

                              . overflows

as if that way
playing with murders
: conjugating the depths

so. burial of sting-fish
. firing a bowl
– one of pigments

( )

the complexity also
. procedures
– for every bond

epiphenomenon
: I pack   .will pack down
– your snow

the caption informs
: "sandstone layer
called white tablet"

Pass as such
little hamlets
proceed by order
. chop the wood
– lay the fire
only a bowl of broth
for dinner
that's how   / what

– slept on the skins

rewrite *Depths*
. in felt-tip
– and copper
without mispelling
but saturated
with the smell

of. the stinking   animal

how to relearn that
. metaphysical

                    as much as pestilential
                    – applied

                  . to the seriousness
                  of a fire   or not

– or not upteenth
. also no matter

                  at the bottom – there. [what sliding
                  game you'll read

                  , it corresponds
                  .. ... – will correspond

now I hear
backwash

      . once
      the ferryman

      . once
      the body

      – fallen
      with lead

            . this
            before the retrocession

            . signing with
            the inheritance agents

and doesn't matter
. who came back   [

      residue
      of permanence

      numerous
      in the vase

      unique
      in the flames

      epic
      under the wind   ]

             breviary
             of children

Market day
. weekly tale
at Père-Lachaise

"rinsings" / composition
with ripe fruits
even still life – there

your smile / there

romain. arugula
. the bus at the stop
– on this / spot you

among fires
– fires down the street –

first considering surface area
. from coastal plants
to bare peet

– I hold
the note

wander my
. fire not   day
– fire not   night

wander   my.
discharged / bony
you.   my despite

                              cure
                up to the right margin.
                   – and your beauty of

                      . Fayoum

fire not
. of endangered species

. water broke
without pain
with

       fire not
       . second ordeal

             . diligent step
             / be it boredom
             navigator ....

– I nearly   forgot
. [traveling shot   on the collar
 of your truck driver's shirt]

                        – but what flashes
                  to break me in?
                              there / inherent

that's why the hurry
not by choice no
. intravenous yes
– quick.   modern

– according to some
. I would have slept
at Val-de-Grâce

cut open / in the tubes
. of one among them

. reassured
for a great number

– and tomorrow?
you understand?

so   "in oneself"
– voice of the *vice-consul*
demand for nothing
. on the lips of the beloved

despite the cocktail
rumours . your boasts
and all.   and all
– I mean to say : a drama

so "of blindness"
that is equivalent to /
mute insistence
coming from your step

where something
smells vaguely
of rotten egg

finally. (sigh)
nor against sustained
nobody unaware
of the painting

who will be the onlooker
. the misuser of the background
– the master of ceremony

silk brushes
. numismatic
– Veronese earth

burnt umber
in the hand
sketch

Further . the putting
into place organizes itself
. slashed barely desired
as Oregon reached

oh Louise ! between
your slow frames
. since I saw them I
would have liked a part

This hymn composed
. of she who loves
– sold. of what in speaking

a slivering where
begins the thus. when.
from an "ideal" cuts itself

well. the reason why
I will always advance
my king   thus

/ perpetually

. from her knee
from her ankle
. the sign

– the womens' dresses
their deportment
– and your knight

face before against

Untitled, 1991
ink and charcoal on blue paper
burnt, 21.5 X 27.9 cm

Louise BOURGEOIS

umber, earth umber
. verse from the book burnt
black

– ink already
of prehistory

while on their backgrounds
. the ancient masters
speak

– before my eyes
tongues made of roots

sea cliff
. low heath

parasol pine
black poplar

dog-rosebush
. lady's-slipper

. head posed face
before against

. a woman spread
– her disaster   apprentice

. the far-off scales
of a sextet

. of your hand recognized
the blurred   gesture
disfiguring the simple

. from the red covering
blood to your   effigy
in front of which

> *no poem*
> *signifies*

no poem
. any longer / signifies
– today but

. this somber varnish
between the thing and us
. face   / to infinity

        ... . also
        only there] . ...

through
their nocturnes

– our hazes
similar

. your frames
denied

there . [*to assail*
– to chamfer

. pound
word

. loosen
ropes

. tighten
keys

    — clavicle
    against clavicle

. there] crossing the greenhouses
there] in the botanical garden

treading on footprints
and clay surfaces

. my weapon

improvised for the scene
of the meeting

: a cherry laurel

Although in dream

the vats his
. of the tanneries
– scented

               the smile of the artisan
              – before me his hands

               one / against the other
              . toward the outside offered out
              – a heart inside

your elbow advancing
idols vanishing
the bodies will be clothed

(cut) in
the indisposition
of rituals

to say in three
like one crosses out
: abolished leaning Pisan

. on the canvas outside
– painted halfway
circumstance would rule

. and otherwise the form
lifted from a story

– hairs   signs stranded
instable depressive

: the face is long
– patterns of migration
adorn the jars

the rounds and the nights
. like engraving
– this art

that bites the flesh
. before the copper

ACKNOWLEDGEMENTS

Special thanks to Eléna Rivera for specific suggestions for modifications and corrections to the translation of *Face devant contre*. Thank you to Norma Cole for her insight about Danielle Collobert.

Grateful acknowledgement is made to the Editions Flammarion, and to Yves di Manno, director of their poetry collection, for the permission to publish an English translation of the original French.

The fifth poem sequence, *Face Before Against*, originally appeared as a SEEING EYE BOOKS chapbook in 2005, edited by Guy Bennett. Excerpts of earlier versions of "overseas" appeared in the online journal, *Double Change* (www.doublechange.com) and the journal, *Verse*.

AUTHOR BIO

Isabelle Garron (b. 1968) is a younger generation French poet who teaches in
Paris. She is the author of *Qu'il faille* (Editions Flammarion 2007), *Face devant contre*
(Editions Flammarion 2002), *Déferlage II* (Editions Les Cahiers de la Seine 2002), and
Le corps échéant (Editions Les Cahiers de la Seine 2000). Garron has also participated
as poet and/or editor in various French journals, including *Petite*, *Action Poétique*,
Action restreinte, *Rehauts*, and *La Polygraphe*. English translations of her poetry have
appeared in *Double Change*, *1913: a journal of forms*, and *Verse*. The chapbook *Face Before
Against*, in Sarah Riggs's translation, was released by Seeing Eye Books in 2005.
Garron's interest in Pierre Reverdy gave rise to a publication of *La Lucarne Ovale* in
its original form (Théâtre Typographique 2001). She is a regular participant with
Jean Daive in the France Culture radio broadcast, "Peinture Fraiche" ("Wet Paint")
on contemporary art.

TRANSLATOR BIO

Sarah Riggs is a poet, translator, and visual artist. She is the author of *Waterwork*
(Chax Press 2007), *28 télégrammes and 60 textos* (éditions de l'Attente, translated by
Françoise Valéry, 2006-7), and *Chain of Miniscule Decisions in the Form of a Feeling*
(Reality Street Editions 2007). She has also published a book of essays, *Word
Sightings: Poetry and Visual Media in Stevens, Bishop, and O'Hara* (Routledge 2002).
The installation of her drawings, *Isibilités*, in collaboration with sound, video and
cuisine, took place at the galerie éof in autumn 2007. A member of Double Change
and director of Tamaas, she has taught at Columbia University in Paris with Omar
Berrada. Together they co-translated Marie Borel's *Wolftrot* (La Presse 2006). She is
at work on a translation of Ryoko Sekiguchi's *Two Markets, Once Again* (Post Apollo,
forthcoming). About *Waterwork*, Ann Lauterbach said: "In five stunning sequences,
Sarah Riggs has created a poetics of elastic migrations that imagines the world as
clusters, skeins, and motions whose innate peril is miraculously saved in the act
of naming..."

OTHER LITMUS PRESS TITLES

Fruitlands, Kate Colby, $12

Danielle Collobert: Notebooks 1956–1978
translated by Norma Cole, $12

Counter Daemons, Roberto Harrison, $15

Animate, Inanimate Aims, Brenda Iijima, $15

Four From Japan: Contemporary Poetry & Essays by Women
translated & with an introduction by Sawako Nakayasu, $14

Inner China, Eva Sjödin
translated by Jennifer Hayashida, $12

The Mudra, Kerri Sonnenberg, $12

Emptied of All Ships, Stacy Szymaszek, $12

Euclid Shudders, Mark Tardi, $12

The House Seen From Nowhere, Keith Waldrop, $15

Another Kind of Tenderness, Xue Di
translated by Keith Waldrop, Forrest Gander, Sue Ellen Thompson,
Theodore Deppe, Stephen Thomas & others, $15

www.litmuspress.org